LETTERS HOME from TURKEY

Lisa Halvorsen

BLACKBIRCH PRESS, INC.

WOODBRIDGE, CONNECTICUT

Published by Blackbirch Press, Inc.
260 Amity Road
Woodbridge, CT 06525

©2000 by Blackbirch Press, Inc.
First Edition

e-mail: staff@blackbirch.com
Web site: www.blackbirch.com

Printed in Singapore

10 9 8 7 6 5 4 3 2 1

All photographs ©Corel Corporation, except pages 14, 15, 16, 20 (left), 24, 25: ©Lisa Halvorsen; page 9 (right): ©Gordon Gahan/National Geographic Society; and page 26: ©Richard T. Nowitz/National Geographic Society.

Library of Congress Cataloging-in-Publication Data
Halvorsen, Lisa.
Turkey / Lisa Halvorsen.
    p.   cm. — (Letters home from . . .)
Includes bibliographical references (p.) and index.
ISBN 1-56711-415-6 (alk. paper)
    1. Turkey—Description and travel—Juvenile literature. [1. Turkey—Description and travel.]
I. Title. II. Series.
DR429.4 .H35 2000
914.961'8044—dc21   00-034246

TABLE OF CONTENTS

Arrival in . . .

Istanbul

We just arrived in Istanbul this morning, but I'm already caught up in the spell of this exotic city. It is an amazing mix of the old and the new. Modern skyscrapers stand next to centuries-old mosques. Well-dressed business people crowd past street vendors and women wearing head scarves and long dresses.

This city is built on two continents—Asia and Europe. It has 10 million people. That's about one-sixth of the total population of Turkey! The country covers 300,000 square miles. It is bordered by the Black Sea to the north, the Aegean Sea to the west, and the Mediterranean Sea to the south. Turkey has been the home of many civilizations since the beginning of time. That's because of its desirable geographic location. It is located close to the point where three continents—Asia, Europe, and Africa—meet.

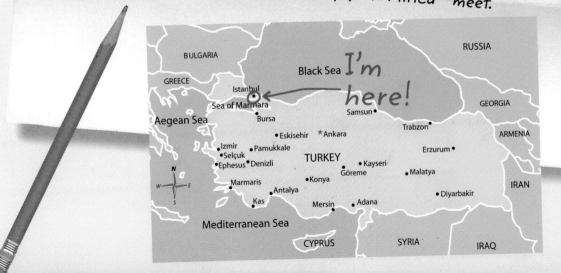

Istanbul

We were awakened at dawn by the muezzin from the nearby mosque. His call to prayer is broadcast over loudspeakers five times a day! About 99% of the Turkish people are Muslims, or followers of Islam.

We walked from our hotel in the Sultanahmet, the city's old section, to Topkapi Palace. It was built in the 15th century and used by many sultans and their families over the next 400 years. I think the palace looks like a fort. A high wall surrounds its many buildings, which include the Imperial Treasury, as well as its courtyards and gardens. The guide said it is the oldest and largest palace in the world!

Terrace of the Favorites, Topkapi Palace

Topkapi Palace

Interior of Ayasofya

Grounds of Ayasofya

We sat outside the palace, watching boats pass under the Bosphorus Bridge, the 5,117-foot suspension bridge that crosses the Bosphorus. This 20-mile-long strait connects the Sea of Marmara to the Black Sea. It separates Europe from Asia.

After lunch we visited Ayasofya. This 6th-century basilica took 10,000 men almost 6 years to build! Its enormous dome is 102 feet across. Although it was built as a Christian church, Ayasofya was later turned into a mosque. Minarets (spires) were added to make it look more like a mosque.

Blue Mosque/Hippodrome

Today we visited the famous Blue Mosque. It is the only mosque in the world with six minarets. Inside we discovered how the mosque got its name. There are more than 20,000 blue tiles!

The Hippodrome once stood in the open square in front of the Blue Mosque. This was where chariot races took place. Today, only part of the curved wall and a few monuments remain.

Blue Mosque

Blue Mosque

Spices in the bazaar

Carpet seller

On the way back to the hotel, we stopped at Kapali Çarşi—the Covered Bazaar—in Beyazit Square. It has more than 4,000 shops under one roof. It is the oldest and largest covered marketplace in the world! It's like a great big maze inside!

I asked a carpet seller to tell us how carpets are made. He told us that most carpets are handmade. Each village weaves its own designs. The wool or silk is dyed with plants to produce the bright colors. Onion skins are used to make green, and sugar beets or cherries are used for red. Blue comes from indigo, and yellow from chamomile or saffron, which is a spice.

9

Misir Çarşi

We also walked through Misir Çarşi, the Egyptian Spice Bazaar, which was noisy and crowded. Many booths had burlap sacks and bins overflowing with brightly colored spices and herbs. You can also buy fruits, nuts, and candy here. I thought the "Turkish delight" was delicious. It's a jellylike candy that's cut in squares and dusted with sugar. Outside, along the waterfront, we stopped to watch some fishermen fry up the day's catch. They cook on small charcoal grills and sell the fish to passersby.

The spice bazaar

Catch of the day

Interior of
Süleymaniye Mosque

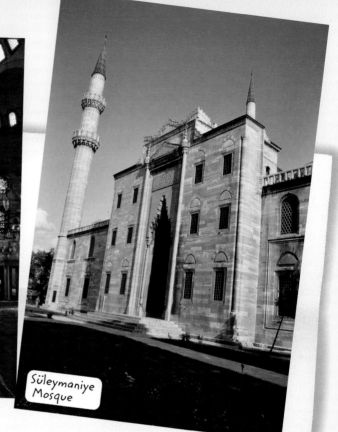

Süleymaniye
Mosque

On our way to the Süleymaniye Mosque, we saw what is left of the massive Roman aqueduct. It was built around A.D. 375 by Emperor Valens to supply water to the palaces.

The mosque, with its four minarets, was built to honor Sultan Süleyman the Magnificent. He reigned from A.D. 1520 to 1566. He was called the Magnificent because he promoted the arts and writing.

Bursa

After a traditional Turkish breakfast of feta cheese, black olives, bread, and tea, we boarded a bus to Bursa. Bursa is about 145 miles south of Istanbul at the foot of Mount Uludag. It is in the middle of a major fruit-growing region. The peaches we bought at the market were sweet and juicy. But I loved the candied chestnuts, too. They are a specialty of the area.

Bursa was the first capital of the Ottoman Empire. No wonder there are so many mosques here! Today we visited the most famous—Yeşil Cami or Green Mosque. Our guide pointed out the green tiles inside that gave the mosque its name.

Entrance to Yeşil Cami

Detail of Yeşil Cami

Entrance to tomb of Ottoman sultan

Tile pattern on Yeşil Türbe wall

Yeşil Türbe (the Green Tomb or Mausoleum) sits in a beautiful garden nearby. Like the mosque, it is covered with green tiles. It was built in 1419 to hold the sarcophagus (stone coffin) of Mehmet I, an early Ottoman sultan. The tomb is highly decorated and is the size of a small house!

After sightseeing all day, we soaked in the hamams, or Turkish baths. The water is heated by thermal springs. It was so relaxing!

Selçuk

We are now in Selçuk on Turkey's western coast. We're visiting the ruins of ancient Ephesus, once one of the five largest cities in the Roman Empire. We walked along marble streets that are more than 2,000 years old! Our guide showed us the agora (marketplace), public baths, and the Marble Way. We also saw the Temple of Hadrian and the two-story Library of Celsus. There's even a huge amphitheater that can seat 25,000 people. I was surprised to learn that it is still used for concerts today!

Library of Celsus

The Marble Way

Basilica of St. John

Grave of St. John

Back in Selçuk, we wandered through the ruins of the Basilica of St. John on Ayasoluk Hill. A guide at the site said that if the basilica were fully restored, it would be the seventh-largest cathedral in the world! Six 95-foot-high cupolas once covered the main aisle! That's huge! We saw the treasury area, the courtyard, baptistry, and the grave of St. John.

Pamukkale

From Ephesus, we traveled inland to Pamukkale. This town is famous for its limestone terraces. I thought they looked like stone waterfalls flowing down the hillside. They are also known as the "cotton castles." For many years, visitors bathed in the pools of warm water. But that caused the limestone to yellow. You can still enjoy the warm mineral water, though. It's piped into many of the swimming pools of nearby hotels. Many people believe the water has healing powers.

We walked to the ruins of Hierapolis, an ancient Roman spa. We saw the remains of the old temple, theater, and the necropolis (city of the dead). Our guide told us that there are hundreds of tombs still to be discovered.

Limestone terraces

Hierapolis

Turquoise Coast

This morning we chartered a gulet in Marmaris to cruise along the Turquoise Coast of the Mediterranean Sea. A gulet is a special wooden sailboat with a pointed bow and a rounded stern. It is traditionally handmade of pine by boatbuilders in towns along the Aegean and Black seas. Our captain explained that "Turkuaz" is the Turkish word for the blue-green color of the water. It became the word "turquoise" in the English language.

Mediterranean coast

Turquoise coast near Mersin

Kaş/Kekova

As we sailed along the rugged coastline, I noticed many little fishing villages along the inlets and bays. I learned that the fishing boats heading out to sea were after mackerel, anchovies, and bonito (tuna). The captain also told us a little about the marine life, including the sea turtles that nest near Ekincik.

We spent the night in the picturesque harbor of Kaş. The next day was market day, so we went into town to wander through the square. People came from many miles around to sell their fruits and vegetables.

Narrow street in Kas

Shops in Kas

At Kekova Island we saw a pirate's cove and an underwater city. The stone houses were once on dry land until an earthquake sunk that part of the island!

We went ashore at Kale. There we climbed the hill to the medieval castle. It has rock tombs cut out of its walls!

Cove near Kekova

Sunken city of Kekova

Antalya

Last night we docked in Antalya. It is so nice to be back on land again! Many Turks, as well as tourists, come here to enjoy the beaches and warm Mediterranean weather. We wandered through the winding narrow streets of the kaleiçi (old city), taking photos of the wooden houses. I also photographed the clock tower, Yivilli Minare (grooved minaret), and Hadrian's Gate. It was built for the Roman emperor's visit in A.D. 130.

Harbor at Antalya

Yivilli Minare

Sis kebap

Sunset in Antalya

Later, we went to an open-air cafe overlooking the harbor for supper. One of my favorite foods is pide. It's like a flatbread pizza with vegetables, ground lamb, sausage, or cheese and egg for toppings. I've also tried sis kebap—grilled lamb on a stick—and dolma, which are vegetables stuffed with a rice or meat mixture.

Our waiter told us that a typical meal starts with soup, followed by a meat and vegetable main course, and then salad. Dolmas are served next. The last course is fruit and dessert, often a milk pudding. Baklava, a honey-soaked pastry with nuts, is usually served as a snack with tea or coffee.

Alanya

Today we arrived in Alanya. Many people visit Alanya for its beaches or to see Damlatas, the "Cave of the Dripping Stones." But its history is also fascinating. It took us an hour to make the winding climb to the 13th-century brick fortress. This double-walled fort has 150 towers! Inside we explored the ruins of mosques, a covered bazaar, and a Byzantine church.

In A.D. 1220, Alaeddin Keykubat captured Alanya for his naval base. The 105-foot-tall, eight-sided red tower (Kizil Kule) was his defense tower. He also built dockyards big enough to service five ships at one time!

The dockyards

Kizil Kule

Konya

We're heading to Konya in central Turkey. This city is considered the religious capital of the country. That's because this is the home of the whirling dervishes. Mevlâna Celaddein Rumi was a Muslim mystic and philosopher. He founded this Islamic order in the 13th century.

The dervishes wear long white belted robes with a high felt turban. They get their name from a religious dance they perform called a Sema. As the music plays, they twirl—arms raised—turning faster and faster until they are in a trance. I'm surprised they don't get dizzy. I did just watching them!

Whirling dervishes

Whirling dervishes

Cappadocia

Cappadocia reminded me of a moon landscape. Our guide explained that millions of years ago a volcano erupted and covered the landscape with molten lava and dust. Wind and rain eroded the soft rock, known as tuff, leaving cones and fairy chimneys. Later, the people of this region carved out churches, monasteries, and homes in the rock.

They also built underground cities to hide from their enemies. We visited Derinkuyu. The city had eight levels. The first level had stables. Other levels had a school, dining hall, food-storage areas, churches, a meeting hall, and living quarters.

Volcanic cones

Fairy chimneys

Church in
Göreme

Church in
Cappadocia

In the Göreme Valley, we entered many of the rock-carved churches and monasteries at the open-air museum. Most are from the 10th to 13th centuries. Their interiors are decorated with beautiful frescoes.

Our guide showed us the nearby Agizkarah Caravanserai. This was one of many rest stops along the Silk Road, a caravan trade route through Asia. It was a place to sleep, pray, buy and sell goods, and rest your animals. A caravanserai was built about every 15 to 26 miles—the distance a camel could walk in a day. About 120 remain in Turkey today.

Ankara

We took a 4-hour bus ride to Ankara, Turkey's second-largest city. As we rode, I read that it was established more than 3,000 years ago at a place where 2 trade routes met. Ankara was once known as Angora.

The modern city of Ankara is built around the hisar. This old fortress and citadel high on the hill marks the site of the original city. We walked up the cobblestoned streets to Hisar Kapisi, the citadel gate. Inside the fortress we saw many old Turkish houses. Along the way we saw many people selling spices, nuts, dried fruits, and all kinds of vegetables.

Spice market

Turkish marketplace

Hittite carving

A shepherd and his flock

According to my guidebook, one-third of Turkey's land is used for agriculture. Most crops and animals are raised on small family farms. Wheat is the main crop, although vegetables—including lentils, beans, sugar beets, and potatoes—make up two-thirds of the production. Many kinds of fruit are grown just about everywhere in the country. Sheep are the main livestock.

A restored 15th-century covered marketplace sits outside the gate. It houses the Museum of Anatolian Civilizations. The museum is a good place to learn about ancient peoples, such as the Hittites and the Ottomans, who left their mark on Turkey.

27

Nemrut Dagi

We flew from Ankara to Gazi Antep where we joined a tour of southeastern Turkey. Our first stop was Nemrut Dagi. The national park is famous for its huge stone statues of gods and kings on a 7,400-foot-tall mountain top. It is Turkey's fifth-highest peak. Mt. Ararat, the resting place of Noah's ark, is the tallest. It is almost 17,000 feet above sea level.

In Turkey, everyone drinks tea. Everywhere we've traveled we've seen men on the streets carrying large urns of tea strapped to their backs. When someone asks for tea, they stop and serve them.

Tea vendor

Sanli Urfa

We stayed overnight in Sanli Urfa, which means "glorious Urfa." Its nickname is the "City of Prophets." Abraham was born in a cave near where the Mevlid Halil Mosque now stands. Several elderly men were praying outside the entrance of the cave.

I took a photo of the sacred carp pools near the Halil-ür Rahman Mosque. Our guide told us a legend about the bad king Nimrod who threw Abraham from the citadel high on the hill into a big fire. As Abraham reached the fire, it turned into water. The ashes became fish. Today many people visit this sacred shrine to Abraham.

The Citadel

Mosque of Abraham

Harran

We continued south to Harran. It is one of the oldest continuously inhabited places in the world. The prophet Abraham spent much of his life here. Many of the 2,300 residents still live in mud-and-brick huts shaped like beehives. The thick walls keep the houses cool in summer and warm in winter.

Although this is a desert region, cotton is one of the biggest crops! That's because a big dam was built to provide water for irrigation (watering crops). We also visited the ruins of the ancient city walls, which date from the 8th century.

The great tower of Harran

The great arch at Harran

Diyarbakir

Diyarbakir is one of the most important cities in southeastern Turkey. It was built on the banks of the Tigris River.

Most of the people in this part of Turkey are nomadic or semi-nomadic—that means they move from place to place. Many grow wheat, rice, vegetables, and grapes in the irrigated valleys. We saw shepherds herding sheep with the help of their Kangal shepherd dog, a breed of Turkish sheep dog.

Tomorrow we head back to Istanbul to fly home. Turkey has sure been a country of contrasts—from its modern buildings to its ancient ruins, and from its turquoise waters to its fertile river valleys and hot, dry deserts.

Farmer cutting wheat

Shepherds herding sheep

Glossary

Aqueduct a channel for water.

Basilica an early Christian church building.

Frescoes paintings made with watercolors on wet plaster.

Kilim a carpet made of a soft wool.

Mausoleum a large tomb, usually a stone building with a places to entomb the dead above ground.

Nomadic having no fixed residence.

Sarcophagus a stone coffin.

Strait narrow passageway connecting two bodies of water.

For More Information

Books

Bator, Robert. Chris Rothero. *Daily Life in Ancient and Modern Istanbul* (Cities Through Time). Minneapolis, MN: Lerner Publications Company, 2000.

Knight, Khadijan. *Islam* (World Religions). New York, NY: Thomson Learning, 1995.

Lyle, Gary. *Turkey* (Major World Nations). New York, NY: Chelsea House Publishing, 2000.

Web Site

Explore Turkey

This site provides information on Turkey's cities, towns, and historical places—www.exploreturkey.com

Index